SPACE
MYSTERIES

ARE UFOs REAL?

 Gareth Stevens
Publishing

BY MICHAEL PORTMAN

Please visit our website, www.garethstevens.com. For a free color catalog of all our high-quality books, call toll free 1-800-542-2595 or fax 1-877-542-2596.

Library of Congress Cataloging-in-Publication Data

Portman, Michael, 1976- author.
 Are UFOs real? / Michael Portman.
     pages cm. — (Space mysteries)
 Includes bibliographical references and index.
ISBN 978-1-4339-8263-7 (pbk.)
ISBN 978-1-4339-8264-4 (6-pack)
ISBN 978-1-4339-8262-0 (library binding)
1. Unidentified flying objects—Juvenile literature. I. Title.
TL789.2P67 2013
001.942—dc23
                                            2012020882

First Edition

Published in 2013 by
Gareth Stevens Publishing
111 East 14th Street, Suite 349
New York, NY 10003

Copyright © 2013 Gareth Stevens Publishing

Designer: Katelyn E. Reynolds
Editor: Therese Shea

Photo credits: Cover, pp. 1, 7 Fuse/Getty Images; cover, pp. 1, 3–32 (background texture) David M. Schrader/Shutterstock.com; pp. 3–32 (fun fact graphic) © iStockphoto.com/spxChrome; p. 4 Comstock/Thinkstock.com; p. 5 tarasov/Shutterstock.com; p. 9 Keystone-France/Gamma-Keystone via Getty Images; p. 11 United States Air Force/AFP/Getty Images; p. 12 Hulton Archive/Getty Images; p. 13 Keystone/Getty Images; p. 15 Al Fenn/Time & Life Pictures/Getty Images; p. 16 Bach01/Wikipedia.com; p. 17 Barney Wayne/Keystone/Getty Images; p. 19 Joshua Roberts/AFP/Getty Images; p. 21 Felix St. Clair Renard/Photographer's Choice/Getty Images; p. 23 NASA/JPL-Caltech; pp. 24, 25 Buyenlarge/Getty Images; p. 27 H. Schweiker/WIYN and NOAO/AURA/NSF; p. 29 Hemera/Thinkstock.com.

Printed in the United States of America

CPSIA compliance information: Batch #CW13GS: For further information contact Gareth Stevens, New York, New York at 1-800-542-2595.

CONTENTS

Words in the glossary appear in **bold** type the first time they are used in the text.

LIGHTS IN THE SKY

There are few things as beautiful and mysterious as the night sky. The glowing moon and the twinkling stars have been a source of wonder for thousands of years. Sometimes, though, the night sky can be a little scary.

For centuries, people have claimed to see strange lights or objects in the sky. Today, we can explain many of these things. However, some things can't be easily explained. What are they? Governments, scientists, and ordinary people have all asked the same question: "Are UFOs real?"

Some people believe that UFOs have been visiting Earth for thousands of years.

5

IT CAME FROM OUTER SPACE!

When most people think of UFOs, they usually think of **aliens** swooping in from outer space. However, the term "UFO" simply means "unidentified flying object." Anything in the sky that we can't recognize, or identify, is a UFO! It doesn't mean that it's an alien spaceship. After all, if we knew that a UFO was a spaceship, it wouldn't be a UFO anymore!

So when did we get the idea that UFOs came from outer space? It was quite recently.

OUT OF THIS WORLD!

Some people don't like the term "UFO" because it makes people think of aliens. They prefer the term "unidentified aerial phenomena," or UAP.

6

"Unidentified aerial phenomena" basically means the same as "unidentified flying object." "Aerial" means "happening in the air," and "phenomena" means "things that are out of the ordinary."

FLYING "SAUCERS"?

On June 24, 1947, Kenneth Arnold was flying his small plane over Washington State. It was a beautiful, clear afternoon. Suddenly, Arnold noticed nine bright objects off in the distance. At first, he thought they were airplanes flying in formation. However, he realized they were moving far too quickly to be planes.

Kenneth Arnold told reporters that the objects flew like saucers skipping across water. The newspapers mistakenly described the objects as "flying saucers." The name stuck, and the UFO craze officially began.

OUT OF THIS WORLD!

A crew on an airline flight claimed to see nine similar objects over Idaho, just 10 days after Kenneth Arnold's sighting.

Kenneth Arnold said the lead object was shaped like a **crescent**. The other eight were shaped like flat disks. This is a photo of UFOs in Ireland in 1950.

ROSWELL

In July 1947, a rancher outside of Roswell, New Mexico, discovered pieces of a metal object in his field. Puzzled by what he saw, he called the police. Soon, officials from the nearby Roswell Army Air Force base took control of the **wreckage**. Their reports called it a flying disk at first. Newspapers printed pictures of military officers holding some pieces.

Later, the military assured the public that it wasn't a flying disk after all. Instead, they said it was only a weather balloon.

OUT OF THIS WORLD!
Years later, some people claimed the military had recovered alien bodies from the crash!

This is a newspaper photo of the Roswell wreckage.
It didn't look like a weather balloon to some people.

11

UFOs TAKE OFF

Shortly after the event at Roswell, hundreds of UFO sightings occurred all over the country. On January 7, 1948, an American pilot named Thomas Mantell Jr. chased a huge metal object through the sky. Shortly afterward, his plane crashed. Newspapers around the country ran stories that said a UFO shot down his plane.

It was later discovered that the US Navy had been performing balloon experiments at the time. Mantell may have flown too high while chasing a balloon and passed out from lack of oxygen.

U.S. NAVY

The military sometimes keeps records of its activities secret. That's why the navy didn't tell anyone about its balloon experiments for a time.

CLOSE ENCOUNTERS

On July 19, 1952, **radar** operators at the airport in Washington, DC, noticed something odd on their screens. Strangely moving aircraft appeared in an area where there weren't supposed to be any—and then took off.

The next night, the aircraft returned. This time, fighter jets were sent after them. One pilot said some UFOs surrounded his plane before speeding off. Despite people claiming to have seen them, the Washington UFOs' appearance on radar was blamed on cold pockets of air in the hot night atmosphere.

OUT OF THIS WORLD!

According to the airport workers, the Washington UFOs moved oddly—differently from other aircraft—and then raced off at an incredible speed!

In this photo, one of the airport workers shows the position of the UFOs that appeared over Washington, DC.

GOVERNMENT INVESTIGATION

The large number of UFO reports caught the attention of the US government. In 1948, the US Air Force began an **investigation**. It's the job of the air force to keep the skies safe. So they had to find out if these sightings were a real danger.

By 1969, the air force had investigated over 12,000 UFO cases. They couldn't find proof of anything unusual or dangerous. They concluded that UFOs weren't from outside this planet, or extraterrestrial. They closed the investigation.

The US Air Force UFO investigation was first called Project SIGN and then Project GRUDGE. In 1952, GRUDGE was replaced with Project BLUE BOOK, which lasted until 1969. They investigated sightings and photos of UFOs such as this.

COVER-UP?

Some people thought the US government wasn't telling the truth about UFOs. They believed the government was trying to hide, or cover up, information. Could it be possible that all the people who claimed to have seen UFOs were wrong?

A small percentage of UFO reports can't be easily explained. That's one reason many people believe that UFOs are real. A few people still believe that UFOs are alien spaceships. Others think that UFOs are top-secret military aircraft.

OUT OF THIS WORLD!

In 1974, an **astronomer** who worked on Project BLUE BOOK, Dr. J. Allen Hynek, created the Center for UFO Studies (CUFOS). CUFOS still investigates UFO sightings.

These people in Washington, DC, demanded that the government publish the reports about the Roswell crash.

POSSIBLE EXPLANATIONS

Our eyes can often play tricks on us. We may think something is moving when it's really standing still. Or, we may think something is close by when it's really far away. These are some of the reasons people mistake ordinary objects for UFOs.

Things such as **meteors**, the planet Venus, airplane or helicopter lights, **satellites**, and weather balloons are mistaken for UFOs. Even valuable tools such as radar can sometimes make mistakes, causing ordinary objects to seem like UFOs.

OUT OF THIS WORLD!

It may seem funny, but birds can be mistaken for UFOs! Sunlight reflecting off some birds can make them look like fast-moving UFOs.

Strange cloud formations can also look like UFOs, more so when the sun shines on them in just the right way.

21

A LONG, STRANGE TRIP

If aliens wanted to visit Earth, they would be in for a very long trip. They had better be prepared to spend years traveling through space. That's because space is incredibly huge. Since the only **intelligent** life in our **solar system** is on Earth, aliens would have to come from planets that are very far away.

It seems puzzling that aliens would travel such great distances and not make contact with us. After such a long trip, wouldn't they at least want to say hello?

OUT OF THIS WORLD!

Scientists are continuing to discover more and more planets outside our solar system. So far, we don't know if any of those planets support life.

Scientists now have powerful tools that can find planets outside our solar system. So far, no aliens or UFOs have been spotted, though.

23

POP CULTURE INVASION

People have long been captivated by the possibility of aliens visiting our planet. In 1938, a radio play based on the H. G. Wells book *The War of the Worlds* aired for the first time. Much of it was made to sound like a real-life news show. Some people thought an **invasion** of **Martians** was really happening!

By the 1950s, movies and books about flying saucers were very popular. In fact, UFOs and extraterrestrials are still a common subject for movies and television shows.

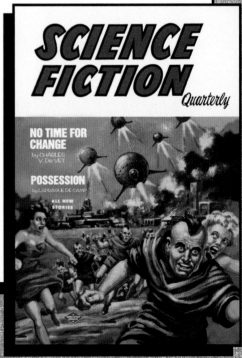

FANTASTIC UNIVERSE

SCIENCE FICTION

NOW
35¢

This book of short stories was published in 1955. However, people are still writing books about UFOs today. How many movies about aliens can you think of?

A KING-SIZE PUBLICATION

25

SIGHTINGS CONTINUE

Today, many people around the world still claim to have seen UFOs. There are even people who say they've been on UFOs! Sometimes large groups of people witness the same UFOs. Other sightings have been caught on video. However, after careful study, most photos and videos turn out to be **hoaxes** or cases of mistaken identity.

Even though the US government no longer investigates UFOs, the case isn't closed for many people. Some have formed groups to conduct their own investigations.

OUT OF THIS WORLD!

The SETI (Search for Extraterrestrial Intelligence) Institute is an organization that looks for signs of life in outer space.

This radio antenna, the largest in the world, is used by SETI and other organizations. It collects and sends signals.

27

YOU DECIDE!

Have you ever seen something you couldn't explain? Perhaps strange lights zigzagging across the sky? Something big and shiny floating in the air? People try to find explanations for things they don't understand. By reading more about UFOs, aircraft, space, and weather, you can decide what you believe.

No one can say for certain if aliens have visited Earth or if there is life on other planets. Maybe someday we'll know for sure. Until then, it's fun to wonder what's really out there!

TOP TEN UFO-SIGHTING STATES

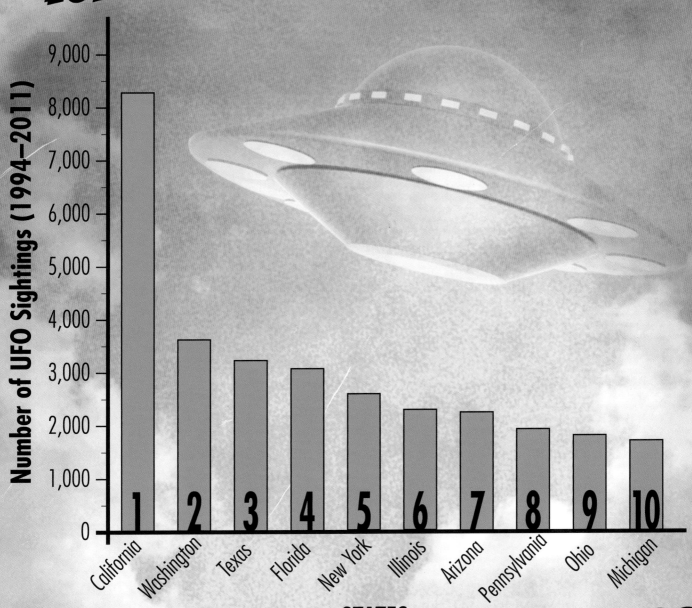

Number of UFO Sightings (1994–2011)

9,000
8,000
7,000
6,000
5,000
4,000
3,000
2,000
1,000
0

1 California
2 Washington
3 Texas
4 Florida
5 New York
6 Illinois
7 Arizona
8 Pennsylvania
9 Ohio
10 Michigan

STATES
according to the National UFO Reporting Center

29

GLOSSARY

alien: a being from another planet

astronomer: a person who studies stars, planets, and other heavenly bodies

crescent: a curved shape, such as the moon when less than half of it is visible

hoax: an act meant to trick someone into believing something that is not true

intelligent: having the ability to learn facts and skills

invasion: the entry of an armed force into an area in order to take control of it

investigation: an ordered search for facts about something

Martian: a fictional creature from the planet Mars

meteor: a mass of rock from space that burns up as it nears Earth

radar: a machine that uses radio waves to locate and identify objects

satellite: an object that circles Earth

solar system: the sun and all objects that circle it, including planets and moons

wreckage: the broken pieces left after something has been damaged

FOR MORE INFORMATION

BOOKS

Herbst, Judith. *UFOs*. Minneapolis, MN: Lerner Publications, 2005.

Mason, Paul. *Investigating UFOs and Aliens*. Mankato, MN: Capstone Press, 2009.

Walker, Kathryn. *Mysteries of UFOs*. New York, NY: Crabtree Publishing Company, 2009.

WEBSITES

History of UFOs
www.history.com/topics/history-of-ufos
Learn more about UFOs by watching videos and reading the most famous stories.

How Aliens Work
science.howstuffworks.com/space/aliens-ufos/alien-physiology.htm
Read about the search for alien life.

INDEX